MW00930277

What did he just say?

Unspeakable Jokes that you shouldn't tell at dinner parties or anywhere else.

What did he just say?
Unspeakable jokes that you shouldn't tell at dinner parties or
anywhere else.
By **Calvin Schumacher**

Printed in the United States of America

Copyright © 2012 **Calvin Schumacher**

Contents

Preface

When I first started researching for jokes I thought that maybe there wouldn't be anything –NEW- out there. Boy was I wrong! After sifting through thousands of internet submissions, I came away with a new sense of things; that there always new and fresh jokes. You can't seem to get away without some of the old ones that have been around forever still making their way into the book. As I wrote these down, I cringed on some, cried on many and just plain looked away from the screen while I typed on a few more. Knowing that some other sick fuck is out there that will think these jokes are funny keeps my fingers moving over the keys. As always, keep the submissions coming and just when you think it's too sick, demented, twisted or just plain wrong to send the joke in, go to http://www.brainspunk.com. Not all submissions make it into the book but we try to jam as many as we can into each volume. Stay tuned for Volume II.

What did he just say?

Chapter 1

What would a joke book be without Black jokes?

What did he just say?

Q: Why do black people smell bad?

A: So blind people can hate them too.

———————

Q: Why couldn't Stevie Wonder read?

A: Because he was black!

———————

Q: Why do they put cotton in pill bottles?

A: To remind black people that they were slaves before they became drug dealers.

———————

Man, I like black people. I think everyone should have one.

———————

Q: What did the 4 year-old black kid ask his father for Christmas?

A: A yo-yo. Nah, I'm just kidding--he has no idea who his father is.

What did he just say?

What's the difference between a nigger and a battery?

A battery has a positive side.

_____

Chinese guy walks into a bar with a black bartender. Chinese guy says, "Give me a jigger, nigger." Black bartender says, "Yo, man, that's not cool. You can't come in here and say that to me." The Chinese guy just smiles from ear to ear. "Give me a jigger, nigger." The black bartender says, "How would you like it if you were behind the bar and I came up and said something like that to you?" The Chinese guy shrugs, "I don't care." So the Chinese guy gets behind the bar, the black bartender goes outside, walks in and says, "Give me a drink, chink!" The Chinese guy says, "I'm sorry, we don't serve niggers in here."

_____

A trucker is driving down the highway with an eighteen wheeler filled with 8-ball style bowling balls when he sees a black kid with a broken bike walking along the side of the road looking for a ride, he stops and says to the kid "I can take you to the next town but you'll have to ride in the back, I can't take hitchhikers, company policy" the kid agrees and gets in the back of the container with

What did he just say?

the bowling balls.

Several miles down the road, the trucker gets pulled over by a redneck cop. Despite the driver's objections the cop insists he needs to check the back of the truck for drugs, so the driver stays in the cab while the cop walks around back and unlatches the back gate.

Suddenly there is a sound of gunfire and the cop comes running back to the front to warn the driver "Holy shit son, you've got a whole load of nigger eggs back there and one of them done hatched and already stole a bike!

_____

Q: What do you do with a black Jew?

A: Put him in the back of the oven.

_____

Q: Why don't Mexicans and black people marry?

A: They're afraid their kids will be too lazy to steal.

What did he just say?

Q: How do you keep a black guy from drowning?

A: Take your foot off his head.

_____

Q: What's long and hard on a black man?

A: Kindergarten.

_____

Q: What does the NAACP stand for?

A: Now Apes Are Called People.

_____

Q: Ever notice there are no black people in The Jetsons?

A: Seems like a good future.

_____

Q: Why are black people so good at dodging bullets?

A: You would too if you spent the first 9 months of your life dodging a clothes hanger.

What did he just say?

Q: What's the most confusing day for a black kid?

A: Fathers day.

_____

Q: Why do you never run over a black man on a bike?

A: It might be your bike.

_____

Q: What's one black man on the moon?

A: A problem.

_____

Q: What's two black men on the moon?

A: A bigger problem.

_____

Q: What's all of the black men in the world on the moon?

A: A problem solved.

What did he just say?

Q: What's the difference between a black man and a bucket of shit?

A: The bucket.

———————————

Q: Why are black people so fast?

A: Because the ones that aren't are in jail.

———————————

Q: What do you call a barn full of black people?

A: Antique farm equipment.

———————————

Q: What do you call a black guy who graduated from medical school?

A: A doctor you fucking racist!

———————————

Q: Why don't black people go on cruise ships?

A: They already fell for that once.

What did he just say?

Q: Why were there no black people in The Flintstones?

A: They were still monkeys back then!

_____

Three males are in an elementary school playground. There's a white, an Asian, and a black kid. The white kid goes, "We've played everything, what's something new we can play?" The Asian says, "How about Bigger Penis? Whoever has the biggest penis wins!" They decide to play and they all pull down their pants. First they look at the Asian kid's penis and it's very small. Then they look at the white kid's penis, it's about medium size but bigger than the Asian's penis. Then the black kid shows his penis and it's bigger than the white kid's and Asian kid's combined. Later that night the black kid says to his mother "Mama, today we played a game called Bigger Penis. Did I win because I'm black?" "NO", says the mother, "It's because you're 32."

What did he just say?

Chapter 2

White jokes! Come get some, Cracker!

What did he just say?

Q: What do you call a white man in a courtroom?

A: Your honor.

_____

Q: How do you know your sister is on her period?

A: Your dad's dick tastes like blood.

_____

Q: What do you call a virgin teenage girl from Alabama?

A: Faster than her brothers.

_____

Q: You know why aspirin are white?

A: You want them to work, don't you?

_____

Q: How do you circumcise a white supremacist?

A: Punch his sister in the jaw.

What did he just say?

A dude in Florida is about to have sex with new wife for the first time, when she tells him that she's a virgin. He stands up, and runs all the way back to his parent's house, 10 miles away. Out of breath, he says "Dad, dad, she ain't never had no sex before!" His father says "Well son, you did the right thing, because if she ain't good enough for her own family, she sure as hell ain't good enough for ours!"

_____

Q: What do you call 300 white men chasing a black man?

A: The PGA tour.

_____

Q: How long does it take for a white woman to take a crap?

A: 9 months.

_____

Q: What's the flat surface to iron jeans on?

A: A white girl's bottom!

What did he just say?

Q: How do you stop five white guys from raping a white woman?

A: Throw them a golf ball.

_____

Q: How many white girls does it take to screw in a light bulb?

A: None, white girls can't screw.

_____

Q: How many white men does it take to screw in a light bulb?

A: One, white men will screw anything.

_____

Q: What did the white man do before his blood test?

A: He studied.

_____

Q: What do u call white people in a bowl of chili?

A: Crackers.

What did he just say?

Q: What did the white woman do after she spilled hot coffee on her legs?

A: File a lawsuit.

――――――――

Q: What do you call 500,000 white guys jumping out of a plane?

A: Snow.

――――――――

Q: What do you call a bunch of white guys in a circle?

A: A Dope Ring!

――――――――

Q: What do you call a bunch of white guys sitting on a bench?

A: The NBA.

――――――――

Q: What do you call a mob of white people in Detroit burning down the city?

A: A hockey victory.

What did he just say?

Q: What do you call a white cop?

A: Police brutality.

_____

Q: What do you call a white man in the ghetto?

A: A victim.

_____

Q: What do you call a white woman with a yeast infection?

A: Crackers with cheese.

_____

Q: What does a white man do when he is unhappy with current government decisions?

A: He writes a letter.

_____

Q: What do a white woman and a tampon have in common?

A: They're both stuck up cunts.

What did he just say?

Q: What does a white woman make for dinner?

A: Reservations.

Q: What is Orange, White and Very Beautiful?

A: A WHITE BOY ON FIRE!

Q: What's the difference between a white man and a snake?

A: One is an evil, cold-blooded, venomous, slimy creature of Satan, and the other is a snake.

Q: What's the difference between a white whore and a white bitch?

A: The white whore would screw everybody in the room and the white bitch would fuck everyone but you.

Q: Why do so many white people get lost skiing?

A: It's hard to find them in the snow.

What did he just say?

Q: Why did white people own slaves?

A: They were not strong enough to pick cotton –
weak bastards.

A skinny little white guy goes into an elevator,
looks up and sees this HUGE black guy standing
next to him. The big guy sees the little white guy
staring at him, looks down and says, "7 feet tall,
350 pounds, 20 inch prick, 3 pound left testicle, 3
pound right testicle, Turner Brown."

The white man faints and falls to the floor. The big
guy kneels down and brings him to, shaking him.
The big black guy asks, "What's wrong with you?"

In a weak voice, the little white guy says, "What
EXACTLY did you say to me?"

The big black dude says, "I saw your curious look
and figured I'd just give you the answers to the
questions everyone always asks me. I'm 7 feet
tall, I weigh 350 pounds, I have a 20 inch prick, my
left testicle weighs 3 pounds, my right testicle
weighs 3 pounds, and my name is Turner Brown."

The small white guy says, "Turner Brown! Sweet
Jesus, I thought you said, "Turn Around!!"

What did he just say?

A seventy-five year old White guy, his hair was completely white, marries a twenty-two year old girl, and she gets pregnant.

Nine months later, he walks into the Maternity Ward. He says to the nurse, "Well, how'd I do?"

The nurse says: "She had twins."

He says, "Heh, heh, heh…well, I guess that goes to show, that even if there's snow on the roof, there can still be fire in the furnace."

She says, "Well, then you'd better change filters. Both of the babies are black."

Q: What's white and twelve inches long?

A: Nothing!

Q: Why shouldn't white people go swimming?

A: Because crackers get soggy when wet.

What did he just say?

Q: Why can't white people jump?

A: Because inbreeding prohibits it.

_____

Q: What do you call a white boy screaming as he's being dragged down the highway behind a black man's pickup truck?

A: A white lane marker.

What did he just say?

Chapter 3

Mazel tov! Jew Jokes!

What did he just say?

Q: What happens when a Jew with a boner walks into a wall?

A: He breaks his nose!

_____

Jewish son walks up to his father and says, "Dad, can I borrow fifty dollars?"

Father says, "Forty dollars? What do you need thirty dollars for? All I have is twenty dollars. How about I give you ten and you give me back five in change?"

_____

Q: Where do you take a Jewish kid with ADD?

A: A concentration camp.

_____

Nazi general walks in to speak to the prisoners of the concentration camps and says to them all:

I have good news and I have bad news! The good news is you will all be repatriated to your mother land in the next few days!!

The bad news? You are going as soap!

What did he just say?

Q: Why do Jews have big noses?

A: Because air is free!

_____

Q: What's the difference between a Jew and a pizza?

A: The pizza doesn't scream in the oven.

_____

Q: What's the difference between Santa Claus and a Jew?

A: Santa goes down the chimney.

_____

A Catholic Priest and a Jewish Rabbi are hanging out at the park. A little boy walks by and the Priest says to the Rabbi, "Wanna fuck him?" The Rabbi replies,"Out of what?"

_____

Q: What's the difference between Hitler and Michael Phelps?

A: Michael Phelps could finish a race.

What did he just say?

Q: What's worse than the Holocaust?

A: 6 million Jews.

_____

Q: What's the difference between a Jew and a boy scout?

A: One comes back from camp.

_____

Q: Why did Hitler commit suicide?

A: He saw the gas bill.

_____

"My grandfather died in a concentration camp...
He fell from the watch tower.

I kid, I kid. He only broke his leg."

_____

Q: What is a Jewish dilemma?

A: Free Pork.

What did he just say?

Hitler is in hell talking to Satan.

Satan: If you could do things all over again what would you change?

Hitler: I would kill 6 million Jews and a clown.

Satan: Why a clown?

Hitler: Zee, no one cares about zee Jews.

_____

Q: Why don't Jews like to eat pussy?

A: It's too close to the gas chamber.

What did he just say?

Chapter 4

Hispanic Jokes!

What did he just say?

Q: Why aren't there any Mexican's in Star Trek?

A: They don't work in the future either.

_____

Q: How many Mexicans does it take to screw in a light bulb?

A: Just Juan.

_____

Q: What do you call two Mexicans playing basketball?

A: Juan on Juan.

_____

Q: What do you say to a Puerto Rican in a 3-piece suit?

A: "Will the defendant please rise..."

_____

Q: A Mexican walks into a wall, which part hits the wall first?

A: The lawnmower.

What did he just say?

Q: How many Mexicans does it take to grease a car?

A: Only one if you hit him right!

Q: Why did the Mexican paint the trash cans red and yellow?

A: So his kids would think they were eating at McDonalds.

Q: Why did the Mexicans lose the Alamo?

A: Because they only brought 2 trucks.

Q: What's the difference between Mexicans and Jesus?

A: Jesus didn't have tattoos of Mexicans all over him.

Q: What's the difference been a Mexican and a bench?

A: The bench can support a family of five.

What did he just say?

Q: Why doesn't Mexico have a good Olympic team?

A: Because anyone who can run, jump, or swim is already in the United States!

———————

One time in Hell, Satan took Hitler to a secret room. Inside was a giant frying pan with a rope in the middle.

"Watch this!" Satan says as he pulls the rope, and 100 Jews fall from the ceiling into the pan and burn alive. "WOW!" Hitler says as he grabs the rope and pulls it over and over.

But one time he pulls it and 100 Mexicans fall into the pan..."What the fuck is this?" Hitler Asked.

"What?" Satan replied, "After a few hundred Jews you need to grease up the pan".

What did he just say?

Chapter 5

Kung Pao Spicy Asian Jokes!

What did he just say?

Q: What do you call a fat Chinese person?

A: A chunk.

_____

Q: What do Virginia Tech and Mount Everest have in common?

A: They're both minus 32 and have killer slopes.

_____

Q: How do you tell the difference between a Chinese person and a Japanese person?

A: A Geiger counter.

_____

They say if you give a Japanese man a fish, he'll eat for a day. If you give a Japanese man a fishing net, he may find the rest of his family.

_____

If your Japanese girlfriend leaves you, don't fret, there are plenty more left in the sea.

_____

I just got a new camera. It was funny how I came across it. Some Japanese tourists asked me to take their picture while I was on the beach. I took the camera and said "Wave!" and they all ran off!

What did he just say?

Q: How do you know an Asian person broke into your house?

A: Your dogs gone, your computers fixed, and they're still trying to back out of the driveway.

What did he just say?

What did he just say?

Chapter 6

Everyone else that got left out..

What did he just say?

All Mexican and Black jokes are the same. Once you've heard Juan you've heard Jamal.

_____

A Black guy, a Muslim guy and a Mexican jump off a cliff, who wins?

Society....

_____

Q: How many ethnic minorities does it take to screw in a light bulb?

A: Enough to reinforce my negative opinion of them.

_____

So a Jew, a nigger and a spic walk into a bar. What does the bartender say?

Get the fuck out.

_____

One day in class, my teacher told me to sit Indian style, so I grabbed a bottle of whiskey and laid down on a curb.

What did he just say?

Q: What do you call a fight between a Mexican and black man?

A: Alien vs. Predator.

_____

Q: What do you call a white guy with a lot of girlfriends?

A: A PLAYER!

Q: What do you call a black guy with a lot of girlfriends?

A: A PIMP!

Q: What do you call an asian guy with a lot of girlfriends?

A: IMAGINARY!

_____

Told by a Native American:

Q: What do snow and white people have in common?

A: They're both white and on my fucking land.

What did he just say?

Polish man is in a lineup for rape; he points at the lady and says "It was her!"

_____

Q: What's white on top and black on the bottom?

A: Society.

_____

Q: What's black on top and white on the bottom?

A: Rape.

_____

An Irishman walks out of a bar.

_____

I was sitting at a traffic light on the interstate highway yesterday, next to a car load of Muslims, when a semi-trailer drove right over the top of their car and killed them all! Wow.... I thought, "That could have been me." So I went and got my truckers license.

Chapter 7

Pedophile Jokes! I didn't know there were so many!

What did he just say?

Q: What's black and blue and doesn't want to have sex anymore?

A: The young Asian boy in the trunk of my car

_____

A man goes to the doctor and says he needs to buy birth control for his 10-year-old daughter. The doctor asks if his daughter is sexually active. The man says, "No, she just lays there like her mother."

_____

Q: How do you make a 10 year old cry twice?

A: Wipe your bloody dick off on her teddy bear when you're done raping her.

_____

My girlfriend texted me the other day and said, "I'm about to watch Titanic - tissues at the ready!"

I replied, "I'm about to watch the Hannah Montana Movie - tissues at the ready!"

She never replied.

What did he just say?

A little girl has to go to the bathroom so she turns to her dad and goes, "Daddy, poo-poo." He goes, "Not now honey, wait like 5 minutes." The little girl really has to go, so she says a second time more urgently, "Daddy! Poo-poo!" and her dad says, "Alright, I'll pull out."

_____

Say what you like about pedophiles, at least they drive slowly past schools.

_____

Little Annie asked her father, "Daddy, can I have a pony?" Her dad says, "Only if you suck my dick." She agrees. Annie then asked, "Daddy, why does your wee-wee taste like poo-poo?" Her dad says, "Because your brother wanted a skateboard."

_____

My girlfriend told me I was a pedophile.

I said, "That's a pretty big word for a seven-year-old."

What did he just say?

Q: What's the best thing about fucking twenty-eight year olds?

A: There are twenty of them!

Q: What's the best thing about fucking a 12 year old girl?

A: Turning her around and pretending she's an 8 year old boy.

Q: What's the difference between a 12 year old and a washing Machine?

A: When you dump your load in a washing machine, it doesn't follow you around for 3 weeks.

A Pedophile and a child are walking towards a dark forest. The child looks up and says "I don't want to go in there. It looks scary!" The Pedophile looks down and says, "You think YOU'RE scared. I have to walk out of there alone."

What did he just say?

On an isolated road winding through the woods, a man comes upon the scene of a terrible car wreck. The car is smashed into a tree and a man and woman are dead, with their heads through the windshield and brains and guts oozing onto the hood. There is also a little girl who apparently was left unscathed without a scratch on her, but was visibly in shock. She had stumbled away from the wreck and is sitting on the side of the road sobbing.

"Oh my God! Little girl, what happened?" said the man.

(Little girl crying) "Wahhhhhh! We were driving... and there was a deer... and we swerved… and then there was a crash.... and blood... and mommy and daddy are dead! Wahhhhhhhhhhh!"

The man looks around, and assesses the horror of the accident and all of the blood and carnage. It was such a miracle that this girl somehow escaped unscathed.

And then he starts undoing his pants.

"Wow" he says, "This just isn't your day."

What did he just say?

Q: What sound does a baby make in a microwave?

A: I don't know, I was too busy jerking off.

_____

A little boy ran up the stairs into his parent's room yelling, "Daddy, Daddy, Daddy! Guess how old I am today!" The father says, "Well, I don't know son ... how old are you?" "I'M SEEEEEEEEVEEN!" "That's great son, now go tell your Grandpa." He runs down the stairs, "Grandpa, Grandpa, Grandpa! Guess how old I am today!" The grandfather looks up from his paper. "Hmm, let Grandpa take a look." The grandfather reaches down the front of the boy's pants and under his underwear. His hard old hands scrap over the boys' penis. He rolls each of the boy's testicles between his thumb and index finger. He pushes further and sticks his middle finger deep into the boys' anus. He flexes his hand. As he pulls his hand out of the boy's pants he pinches the tip of the boys' penis to the point where the boy cries "Ow!" The grandfather says, "You're seven." The boy, "Yeah Grandpa, how could you tell?" The grandfather said, "I heard you tell your father."

What did he just say?

Q. What's the worst part of raping an eight-year-old boy?

A. Getting blood all over your clown suit.

_____

Q: Why did Michael Jackson dangle his son over the balcony?

A: To shake the cum off.

_____

Pedophiles are fucking immature assholes.

_____

"So I was fucking this chick in the ass in my clown suit, when she turns to me and says, "a clown suit, isn't that a bit ostentatious?' And I said, "Ostentatious, isn't that a big word for an 8 year old?'"

Chapter 8

Jokes for the Handi-Capable!

What did he just say?

If a mentally challenged midget is late to an appointment, can you justifiably call them "a little tardy".

_____

What did the blind deaf girl get for Christmas?

Cancer.

_____

Q: What's the difference between Sarah Palin's mouth and her vagina?

A: Only half the things that come out of her vagina are retarded.

_____

Q: Why did the little girl fall off the swing?

A: She had no arms.

_____

Q: What do you call a kid with no arms, leukemia, and an eye patch?

A: Names.

What did he just say?

Q: How do you turn a fruit into a vegetable?

A: AIDS.

_____

Q: What's the hardest part of a vegetable to eat?

A: The wheelchair.

_____

Q: What do you call an epileptic in a bathtub?

A: A washing machine.

_____

Q: What's better than winning a gold medal at the Special Olympics?

A: Not being fucking retarded.

_____

Q: Why does Helen Keller only masturbate with one hand?

A: So she can moan with the other.

What did he just say?

Q: How did Helen Keller's parents punish her?

A: They left the plunger in the toilet.

_____

Q: How did Helen Keller's parents punish her?

A: Move the furniture around.

_____

Q: How did Helen Keller's parents punish her?

A: Glue doorknobs to the walls.

_____

Q: How did Helen Keller's parents punish her?

A: Put her in a circular room and tell her to sit in the corner.

_____

Q: Why didn't Helen Keller scream when she fell off a cliff?

A: She was wearing mittens.

What did he just say?

Q: Did you know Helen Keller had a horse?

A: No. Neither did she.

_____

Q: What was Helen Keller's favorite color?

A: Velcro.

_____

Q: How did Helen Keller lose her hand?

A: She tried to read a stop sign while going 45 mph.

_____

Q: How did Helen Keller drive?

A: One hand on the wheel and one hand on the road.

_____

Q: Why is Helen Keller's leg yellow?

A: Because her dog is blind too.

What did he just say?

Q: Why did Helen Keller's cat commit suicide?

A: You would too if your name was Uhnnnnnnhhh.

_____

Q: Why did Helen Keller's dog run away?

A: You would too if your name was eughhahhh.

_____

Q: How do you keep Helen Keller busy for an hour?

A: Tell her to read a basketball.

_____

Q: What's the opposite of Christopher Reeve?

A: Christopher Walken.

_____

A quadriplegic girl is lying on the beach, when an attractive young man sat down next to her. They got to talking, and after a while she shyly says to him, "You know, I've never been kissed." After a moment's thought, the young man bent over and kissed her. "Now you've been kissed," he says.

What did he just say?

Then she says, "I've never seen a penis." The young man is a bit more hesitant about this, but after a minute he pulls off his trunks and shows her his dick. "Now you have," he says.

Encouraged, the girl says quietly, "I've never been fucked."

Whereupon the boy immediately picks her up and throws her into the raging ocean, and yells, "Now you're fucked!"

———————

Q: How did Helen Keller's parents punish her?

A: Made her read stucco.

———————

Q: Why couldn't anyone hear Helen Keller when she fell off a cliff?

A: She was wearing mittens.

———————

Q: What do a warm beer and a retarded newborn baby have in common?

A: The first thing to do is blow the head off.

What did he just say?

What did he just say?

Chapter 9

9/11 Jokes.

What did he just say?

Q: What did the hotdog vendor at the bottom of the World Trade Center say?

A: Who ordered the 2 jumbo's?

_____

Guy walks into a bar and orders a Bin Laden. The bartender asks, "What's a Bin Laden?" Guy says, "Two shots and a splash of water."

_____

Q: What's grey, white and black and looks good on a cop?

A: The World Trade Center.

_____

Knock Knock!

Who's there?

9/11.

9/11 who?

YOU SAID YOU'D NEVER FORGET!

What did he just say?

The thing about 9/11 jokes are that they are just plane wrong.

_____

Q: What's the difference between the New York Mets and the World Trade Center?

A: The Mets collapse every September.

_____

You've got it good in America. We have to get to work by car or train, but in the United States, you can take a plane straight into the office!

_____

Q: What was the most inappropriate thing said on 9/11?

A: JENGA!

_____

Q: Who were the world's fastest readers?

A: The World Trade Center employees. Some went through over a hundred stories in seconds.

What did he just say?

Chapter 10

Sexist Jokes.

What did he just say?

Q: Why should you never buy a woman a watch?

A: There's a clock on the stove.

_____

Q: What do you do if your woman comes out of the kitchen complaining?

A: Shorten her chains.

_____

Q: Why do women get periods?

A: Because they FUCKING DESERVE IT!

_____

Q: How long does it take for a woman to have an orgasm?

A: Who cares.

_____

If I had any less respect for women, I'd have to be a Muslim.

What did he just say?

Q: What do you say to the feminist with no arms or legs?

A: Nice tits, Bitch.

_____

Q: Why can't Helen Keller drive?

A: Because she's a woman!

_____

Q: What do you do when your dishwasher stops working?

A: Punch her.

_____

Q: Do you know how to give a woman more freedom of speech?

A: Take your dick out of her mouth!

_____

Q: What do you call the useless skin around the vagina?

A: The woman.

What did he just say?

Q: How many feminists does it take to change a light bulb?

A: Trick question, feminists can't change anything.

_____

Q: What do you tell a woman with two black eyes?

A: Nothing. She's already been told twice.

_____

Q: How are women similar to condoms?

A: They're either on the end of your dick or in your wallet.

_____

Q: What do you call a woman who doesn't have dinner ready on time?

A: An ambulance.

_____

Q: What do the battered women of the world have in common?

A: They never fucking listen.

What did he just say?

You mean, you can batter women?

I've been eating them plain.

_____

Q: What do you call a woman with one black eye?

A: A quick learner.

_____

Q: What is the first thing a woman should do after leaving the shelter for battered women?

A: The Dishes. If she knows what's good for her!

_____

Q: Why where shopping carts invented?

A: So women could learn to walk on their hind legs.

_____

Q: How do you turn a dishwasher into a snow blower?

A: Hand the bitch a shovel.

What did he just say?

Q: Why haven't we sent women to the moon?

A: It doesn't need cleaning...

Chapter 11

Homosexual Jokes!

What did he just say?

Two condoms are walking down the street and pass a gay bar. One says to the other, "Hey, want to go in and get shit faced?"

_____

Q: What is the difference between a refrigerator and a gay guy?

A: The refrigerator doesn't fart when you take the meat out.

_____

Q: How do you get 4 fags on a bar stool?

A: Turn it upside down

_____

Q: How do you know if your best friend is gay?

A: His dick tastes like shit.

_____

Q: Why do you duct tape a hamster?

A: So it doesn't explode when you fuck it.

What did he just say?

Q: How do you get a fag to fuck a girl?

A: Shit in her cunt.

_____

Q: What's the hardest part about learning to rollerblade?

A: Having to tell your dad you're gay.

What did he just say?

Chapter 12

Dead Babies and more!

Q: What's the difference between a truck full of babies and a truck full of bricks?

What did he just say?

A: You can't use a pitchfork on the bricks.

_____

Q: What's purple covered in pus and squeals?

A: A peeled baby in a bag of salt.

_____

A pregnant woman was at the hospital giving birth to her baby. The delivery was almost complete, and at long last, the doctor held up the newborn, cut the umbilical cord, and took a moment to look the baby over. Then without missing a beat, the doctor threw the child against a nearby wall with all of his might. The mother watched in shock as the baby slid to the floor with a sickening thud.

The nurses and orderlies stood-by aghast as the doctor proceeded to dribble the newborn around the room like a soccer ball before finally passing the baby through the door into the hall with a mighty kick. Everyone, including the fatigued mother, chased the doctor into the hall just in time to see him scoop up the infant and run down the corridor, stopping just long enough to body check the child into the wall every so often.
At the end of the hall, the doctor gave a mighty leap and slam-dunked the baby into a nearby trashcan, giving himself a loud roar of approval.

What did he just say?

Finally the now quite large awe-struck crowd caught up with the doctor. The mother was distraught and burst into tears.

"Why? Why in the name of God did you do that to my baby?", she cried.

The doctor replied, "Just kidding! It was already dead!"

_____

Q: How do you get a baby into a bowl?

A: Blender.

_____

Q: How do you get a baby out of the bowl?

A: Nachos.

_____

Q: How many dead babies can you fit in the trunk of a car?

A: 46.

Q: What's the difference between a dead baby and an apple?

What did he just say?

A: I don't cum on an apple before I eat it.

_____

Q: What's the difference between a baby and a watermelon?

A: One is fun to hit with a hammer, and the other is a watermelon.

_____

Q: What does a micro-waved baby look like?

A: I don't know, I close my eyes when I masturbate.

_____

Q: Why can't you fool an aborted baby?

A: Because it wasn't born yesterday.

_____

Two expecting women are sitting down knitting at a pre-natal class. After a while the first woman reaches into her bag and brings out a bottle of pills and knocks a few back. Second woman asks "Are you taking those for the baby?" First woman says "Yeah, Vitamin C and Iron supplements" They continue to knit for a while and then the second

What did he just say?

woman reaches into her bag and brings out a bottle of pills and knocks a few back. First woman says "Oh, so you are taking supplements as well?" Second woman says "No - it's Thalidomide - I can't knit sleeves."

_____

Q: What's the difference between a baby and a trampoline?

A: You take off your boots to jump on a trampoline.

_____

Q: What's the difference between a Ferrari and a sack of dead babies?

A: I don't have a Ferrari in my garage.

_____

Q: How many dead babies does it take to paint a fence?

A: It depends on how hard you throw them.

Q: What's the difference between a baby and a bowling ball?

What did he just say?

A: One gets thrown in the gutter and the other ones a bowling ball.

_____

Q: What's pink and red and climbs up your leg?

A: A home sick abortion.

_____

Q: What's pink and blue and sits in the corner?

A: A baby in a plastic bag.

Q: What's green and sits in the corner?

A: The same baby 2 weeks later.

_____

Q: What's the difference between a truck load of bowling balls and a truck load of babies?

A: You can't unload the bowling balls with a pitchfork.

Q: What's grosser than 10 dead babies in a dumpster?

What did he just say?

A: One baby in 10 dumpsters.

_____

Q: What's the difference between a baby and a bag of cocaine?

A: Eric Clapton would never let a bag of cocaine fall out a window.

_____

Q: What's red and bubbly and scratches on the glass?

A: A baby in a microwave.

What did he just say?

What did he just say?

Chapter 13

Necrophilia Jokes. A moment of silence for the dead please.

What did he just say?

Q: What's the difference between rape and necrophilia?

A: About 5 minutes.

_____

Q: What's the worst part about fucking your grandma?

A: Banging your head on the coffin lid.

_____

A man goes to a brothel and walks up to the clerk at the front desk. The man says "I would like to buy some entertainment for the night." The clerk replies, "I would recommend Jessica. She is on the 3rd floor, room 7. She is $250 for the night." The man replies, "That's Outrageous! I can't pay that!" The clerk then suggests Vanessa on the 2nd floor. He tells the man that she is $150 for the night. The man says "Listen I have $60. That's all I can pay." The clerk says "Go down the left hallway here and she will be in the last door on the left." The man pays and goes to the room. The girl is there and already on the covers naked. She is extremely hot! He rips his pants off and starts going to town. About 10 seconds after he starts in on her she starts foaming at the mouth and her eyes roll up. The man screams and runs out to the

What did he just say?

clerk. He tells him what happened. The clerk immediately grabs the phone and makes a call. He says "Yeah, Tony? The dead one's full again."

_____

One evening Bob comes into the local pub, sees a couple of friends and goes and sits down with them. Bob is very agitated. "Listen to what happened to me last night!" he says.

"I was on my way home and stopped at the train tracks waiting for a train to go by. Just before it gets there this gorgeous woman out for a jog tries to beat it, but she trips and falls head first right over the tracks. Well, I had only seconds to save her, so I jumped out of my car, grabbed her ankles and pulled her off the tracks just as the train got there. Well, let me tell you, she was so appreciative that we went straight back to my place and we did it all night long and in just about every position. She even let me do anal sex on her!"

"Whoa," says Bob's friends, "Amazing!" Then one of them asks, "Did she give you a blow job, too?"

"Nah," says Bob. "I never did manage to find her head."

What did he just say?

Two gay guys are standing outside a cemetery, and one says to the other "Hey, wanna go inside, crack open a couple of cases and suck back a few cold ones?"

───────────

So I was eating out my grandma, right? All of a sudden, I started to taste donkey semen. I was like, "Aw, Grandma, that's how you died?"

───────────

John, Mary, and Steve got stranded on a remote island. They are stranded for months and months and eventually give into their urges. John and Steve each start casually having sex with Mary. This goes on for months as they live on their remote island, but eventually Mary starts to become depressed. She starts to feel like she is just a sex object for the two men, so she commits suicide. A few days pass and John and Steve, once again, give into their urges. They start to do something that some religious folk may say is unnatural or disgusting. This goes on for a few weeks, but finally they decide that it's just too wrong and they have to stop... So they bury Mary.

What did he just say?

Q: Why was the necrophiliac so upset?

A: Some rotten cunt split on him.

What did he just say?

What did he just say?

Chapter 14

These are just wrong.

What did he just say?

Q: What do spinach and anal sex have in common?

A: If you were forced to have it as a kid, you'll hate it as an adult.

_____

A man's wife is dying of cancer in the hospital and she only has a little while left to live. The man crawls into the hospital bed to hold his wife, and whispers to her, asking if there is anything he can do for her. She says that she wished that they had tried anal sex at least once, and that she didn't want to die without having tried it. The man is shocked, but he decides to accommodate his wife's dying wish. After a few minutes they are finished, and the man gets up out of the bed to go clean up.

When he comes out of the bathroom, he notices that his wife looks different. In fact, she looks better than she has in months. Before he can say anything, his wife sits up and says, "I feel wonderful!" She feels so good that she gets out of the bed and starts walking around the room. She tells her husband that she believes that she's cured, and that is was the anal sex that cured her!

They are both very happy, until a look of shock

What did he just say?

comes over the man's face. He sits down in a chair and starts to cry. His now-perfectly-healthy wife asks, "Honey! What's wrong!?" He looks at her in anguish and says brokenheartedly, "I could have saved my Dad!!!"

_____

A man and a woman are sitting at the bar one night, drinking their problems away. After a time, the man decides to ask the woman, "What's the matter, you seem really down?" The woman responds, "Well, it's just that my husband left me." The man looked surprised as the woman was quite attractive and asked "Why would he leave you?" The woman replied, "He said I was too kinky in the bedroom." Immediately the man's eyes lit up in shock at her answer. "My wife actually just left me for the same reason," he told her, and it was the truth. The two of them get to talking and eventually she invites the man to her home. They enter her bedroom, and the woman instructs the man to take a seat on the bed, that she is going to 'get ready' in the other room. The woman proceeds to attire herself in a leather corset, complete with whip, chains, and ballgag. She heads to the pantry and grabs a bottle of whipped cream and some Tabasco sauce. The woman then reenters the bedroom to see the man putting on his coat about to walk out the door. The woman

What did he just say?

exclaims, "What's the matter? I thought you were kinky!" to which the man replied, "Lady, I just fucked your dog and shit in your purse, I'm done here."

_____

This guy is grocery shopping when an extremely attractive woman walks up to him.

"Excuse me," she says "I know this is rather forward, but... I think you're the father of one of my children."

The guy goes pale as a sheet. "Oh, geez. Are you sure?"

"Yes I'm positive I remember you". The woman is extremely attractive with large breasts, penetrating eyes and pouting, tender lips. The guy tries to remember where he knows her from and then it hit him.

"Oh my god," he says "You aren't... the dancer from John's bachelor party three years ago? The one who rubbed peanut butter on my balls and had the dog lick it off on stage? I remember we went back to your apartment, where you blindfolded me and made me fish a soggy banana out of the toilet bowl with my teeth, and then we

What did he just say?

fucked while your roommate drilled me in the pooper with a strap-on. I'm not surprised you got pregnant; I came so hard I remember a little even squirted out your nose!"

"Actually," the woman said, "I meant that your son Jeremy is in my English class."

———————

The day after he had lost his wife scuba diving, two grim-faced policemen paid Mr. Smith a visit. "We're sorry to disturb you at this hour, Mr. Smith, but we have some information concerning your wife. Actually, we have some bad news, some pretty good news and some really great news. Which would you like to hear first?"

Fearing the worst, Mr. Smith asked for the bad news first.

"We're sorry to inform you, sir," the policeman said, "we found your wife's body in the San Francisco Bay this morning."

"Oh, my God!" said a distraught Mr. Smith. "What's the good news?"

What did he just say?

"When we pulled her up," said the policeman, "she had two five-pound lobsters and a dozen crabs on her."

"What?" a confused Mr. Smith exclaimed. "So, what's the great news?"

The officer replied, "We're going to pull her up again tomorrow."

_____

Q: Why is a Rubik's' Cube and a cock so similar?

A: Because the longer you play with it, the harder it gets.

_____

My mom walked in on me jerking off, then started yelling at me! Not because I was violently tugging on my dick, but because I was holding a picture of her!

_____

Bill has worked in a pickle factory for several years. One day he confesses to his wife that he has a terrible urge to stick his penis into the pickle slicer. His wife suggests that he see a therapist to talk about it, but Bill vows to overcome this rash desire on his own. A few weeks later, Bill returns

What did he just say?

home absolutely ashen. His wife asks, "What's wrong, Bill?" "Do you remember how I told you about my tremendous urge to put my penis into the pickle slicer?" His wife gasps, "My God, Bill, what happened?" "I got fired." "No, Bill -- I mean, what happened with the pickle slicer?" "Oh, she got fired, too."

What did he just say?

Chapter 15

Losing your Religion? You won't find it here.

What did he just say?

Q: Why can't Jesus eat M&M's?

A: Because they keep falling through the holes in his hands.

_____

Q: What's the difference between Jesus and a portrait of Jesus?

A: It only takes 1 nail to hang a portrait of Jesus.

_____

Q: Why did Jesus die on the cross?

A: Because he forgot the safe-word.

_____

Jesus walked into an Inn. He tossed three nails on the counter and said, "Can you put me up for the night?"

_____

Q: How did Jesus cross the road?

A: He was nailed to the chicken.

What did he just say?

Q: What's the difference between Jesus and a hooker?

A: The look on their face when they're getting nailed.

————————————

Q: How are the Bible and a Penis similar?

A: Priests try to shove them both down little boy's throats.

————————————

Q: What's the difference between a priest and zits?

A: Zits don't come on your face until you're 13.

What did he just say?

What did he just say?

Chapter 16

We could never leave the celebrities out…

What did he just say?

Q: Did you hear about the Macho Man's next opponent?

A: It's the Undertaker.

───────────

Q: Why did Princess Diana cross the road?

A: She wasn't wearing her seatbelt.

───────────

Princess Diana was the first person to die from Car-Pole-Tunnel Syndrome

───────────

Q: What were Michael Jackson's last words in the ambulance?

A: "Take me to the children's hospital."

───────────

Q: Where does Princess Diana stay in Paris?

A: Anywhere she can crash.

What did he just say?

Steve Irwin died like he lived, with animals in his heart.

What did he just say?

What did he just say?

Chapter 17

They just didn't fit anywhere else...

What did he just say?

Q: Why does Dr Pepper come in a bottle?

A: His Wife's dead.

_____

My girlfriend is a porn star.

She is going to be so pissed off when she finds out.

_____

A gynecologist has a midlife crisis and takes night classes to become a mechanic.

She's really nervous the night of the final, so she studies real hard and hopes for the best.

When the grades are posted, she freaks out because her grade says 150% and she assumes it was an error so she goes to see the instructor.

He explains it's no error. "You took apart the engine perfectly, every nut, every bolt, you pulled it all apart without breaking anything. That got you 50%

Then you put it all back together perfectly. It actually ran better than before you started, so I gave you 50% for that.

What did he just say?

You got a bonus 50% for doing it all through the muffler."

_____

Q: How do you stop a dog from humping your leg?

A: Suck its dick.

_____

So, a baby seal walks into a club....

_____

What did the apostrophe in the plural say?

Nothing. There are no apostrophes in plurals.

_____

Q: What's the difference between menstrual fluid and sand?

A: You can't gargle sand.

_____

Q: Why aren't there any jokes about Jonestown?

A: Because the punch-lines would be too long.

What did he just say?

A Capitalist, a Conservative and a Socialist arrive at the bakery right as a dozen cookies come fresh out of the oven.

The Capitalist quickly snatches Eleven of them and then turns to the Conservative to warn him that the Socialist wants to eat the remaining cookie.

_____

Q: Three tampons are walking down the street, small, medium, and large. You wave to them, which one waves back?

A: None of them, they're all stuck up cunts.

_____

How many dead hookers can I fit in my garage?

Two more if I move my bike.

_____

Knock Knock.

Who's there?

Banana.

Banana who?

What did he just say?

Orange you glad I didn't say banana.

_____

Q: Why did cavemen drag their women around by the hair?

A: Because if you drag them by their feet, they get filled up with dirt!

_____

Q: What's the pussy of an 80 year old woman taste like?

A: Depends.

_____

Q: What's the difference between a pimp and Santa Claus?

A: Santa stops after three Ho's.

What did he just say?

What did he just say?

Chapter 18

Jokes for our Third World friends.

What did he just say?

Q: How do you kill 100 flies at once?

A: Punch a Somalian in the face.

_____

Q: What do you call an Ethiopian with a yeast infection?

A: A quarter pounder with cheese.

_____

Q: How do you get an Ethiopian pregnant?

A: Cum on her back and let the flies do the rest.

_____

Q: What's the difference between an Ethiopian and a pair of pants?

A: A pair of pants only has one fly on it.

_____

Q: How long does it take a Pakistani woman to make a bomb?

A: 9 months.

What did he just say?

Q: Have you ever had Ethiopian food?

A: Neither have they.

_____

Q: What's the best part of getting head from an Ethiopian chick?

A: You know she'll swallow.

What did he just say?

Chapter 19

Rape Jokes? Really?

What did he just say?

Q: What's the most effective pickup line you know?

A: Don't make me turn this rape into murder.

_____

Rape is just a compliment in 3-D.

_____

Q: What is the difference between an onion and a hooker?

A: I never cried when I cut a hooker.

_____

Q: What do 5 of 6 people always agree on?

A: Gang rape.

_____

I called the rape helpline last night.

It was useless, they wouldn't even tell me how to shut her up.

Made in the USA
San Bernardino, CA
20 December 2013